Dare to be Different

Discovering Your God Given Uniqueness!

Mirron Noble

3G Publishing, Inc.
Loganville, GA 30052
www.3gpublishinginc.com
Phone: 1-888-442-9637

First published by 3G Publishing, Inc. May, 2016

ISBN: 9781941247310

Printed in the United States of America

In Memory Of
My Spiritual Mentoring Midwives and Closest Friends:
Dr. Dorothy Exume'
Missionary Pearl Williams
Evangelist Arlene Johnson
Mother Christine Grayson

Contents

Foreword

My desire and prayer for every reader of this book is that you will begin to celebrate the God-given differences that make you who you are. Perhaps before reading this book, the enemy of our purposes and destiny has caused you to despise the very attributes that make you a unique and one-of-a-kind vessel of the Creator. I pray and hope that you will begin to embrace yourself with all of your differences and realize that God has divinely equipped you to be a building block in His kingdom. Your brick is unlike any other and no one can take your place or replace you. I trust that when you come away from this book, you will be enlightened with a new understanding of who you really are. I know that you will become sincerely inspired to take on the challenge of looking at your differences from a totally different perspective. Your differences are the Great Master Builder's chisel to shape you to fit perfectly into His will and purpose. So start the journey of daring to be the different servant of God that He has created you to be!

To God be the Glory
Dedication

This book is dedicated in memory of my parents, Pastor Henry Walter Noble and my loving, unique, one-of-a kind mother, Mother Lottie M. Noble, for the legacy of godly living that they both left to me.

Acknowledgments

With Special Thanks:

To my dear children, Stephanie, Stacey, Spencer, Stephen, and Samuel, for their love, support, and encouragement.

To my friend and mentor, Fannie Aidoo, who spoke prophetically concerning the writing of this book years before it was conceived. Thanks for all of your intercessory prayers, encouragement, and for just being there whenever I needed you.

To my daughter-in-love, Keisha, who has a unique way of always making me feel so special.

To my god-children, the Jennings Family, I truly thank God for each of you. Never could have made it without you.

To my Pastor, Bishop Norman O. Harper, for all of the fresh and anointed messages that he preaches that help to keep me uplifted, focused, and motivated.

Chapter 1

Dare to Give Birth to Your Purposes

Little did I know several years ago that when the Lord first made me aware of these mere four words [dare to be different] that this would be the conception of a whole new life for me! These words became the womb that carried my destiny, and I began to perceive that I was the only one who could determine the outcome of this birth.

With this being the case, I learned to embrace and accept the first of many of life's challenges. Shortly thereafter, I discovered that no matter how painful the challenges became, they would later give birth to purposes.

Yes, the Word of God declares to us that we are fearfully and wonderfully made. Based on this divine knowledge we become aware at some point in our lives that each of us is different. Even medical science has proven that no two people are exactly the same. Nevertheless, so many of us struggle most, if not all, of our lives to either be like someone else, to be someone else, to be what others want or expect us to be, or with being just plain unhappy or dissatisfied with who we are.

We all have met someone who is obsessed with what they consider a personal flaw of themselves. If they are short, they wish that they were taller or vice versa. The obsessions can go on and on and can even become very extreme. If you haven't met anyone that fits this description then chances are you are one of those persons.

Society has dictated to us many reasons why we should try to be something or somebody else. We in turn, have made many of society's industries wealthy by taking them up on their solution to fix us. Hardly anyone is happy just being themselves, it seems. Those who are, if the truth be told, have had many of life's miscarriages before finally giving birth to the real and true individual that the creator made them to be.

Even I must confess that the Lord had to be very patient with me before I was to completely grasp the absolute essence of what He was trying to bring out of me and at the same time place inside of me. Season after season of being impregnated with life's array of troubles is what brought me to a place of total submission to the master's plan of pre-natal care.

I guess you can say that I came into this world with what I would call a challenged difference: weighing in at 11 pounds and 13 ounces at birth (a little shy of being a 12 pound infant)! Surely with such a unique beginning I must be endowed with many special and wonderful gifts and talents. I should take time here to say, "Thank God for my mother who dared to give birth!"

As I grew up I soon found out that in order to tap into any special and wonderful gifts, I had to first become best friends with the person that I saw in the mirror every day. I quickly learned that uniqueness is always accompanied with challenges.

How often did I have to endure the contractions of awareness that you only need approval and permission from you to be you; along with the fact that you can be very sure that you are truly loved by God. The Creator of you will love you unconditionally and His love will outgrow and outlast any unique challenges that come from daring to give birth.

This brings me to a major life-changing experience that has taught me a very valuable lesson. It is one that keeps me grounded, and places me in the path of people that have learned the same lesson.

Are you ready? Well, here it is: you are only as special as you think you are not. No, I did not make a mistake. I did say, "as you think you are NOT."

Let me explain what I mean by this. Truly special people do not consider themselves to be special. The reason for this is because they are so involved and preoccupied with making other people feel special. They unselfishly share themselves with others so that they too can dare to give birth to their purposes. They even tend to put themselves on the back burner. What is even more outstanding about these rare individuals is that they expect nothing in return. These wonderfully created beings just seem to believe that this is what everybody has been placed in this world to do so they just become self-made coaches. I was very blessed to have a few of these special people assist me along the way throughout the birthing of my purposes.

However, before I actually obtained a degree in that lesson of life, from a child, I found myself often times comparing myself with others. I would ponder intensely over the differences between me and other family members as well as people around me. I was not aware at the time that God had picked me out to be somewhat over-conscious of differences between me and others. This was not to make me feel inferior, but to make me more appreciative of how unique He had made me for His purposes.

I have many vivid memories of thinking "Wow! I wish I could", or "I wish I had"….or just trying to figure out why I was like I was!

But all was not a life of constant regret and despair. Growing up in a pastor's home, there were many rules of dos and don'ts. Consequently, the things about me that made me different actually made it easy for me to submit to the don'ts that other children growing up in a strict Christian home struggled with.

I remember always wanting to honor God by honoring my father and mother. I never wanted to cause them any grief by departing from the way they had trained me up to go. Not realizing it then, but I was already daring to be different. At a very early age I had stumbled into a journey of pre-ordained challenges that were tailor made to work together for my good! I must confess that at times it seemed as if there were no good to come at all.

Naturally children are open, honest, and straight to the point. In spite of being an introvert and extremely shy, I possessed those same natural child-like characteristics. The problem with that was, as I grew into an adolescent, I discovered that mindset was not a very popular choice of character.

Even before salvation, it was difficult for me not to be honest, open, and straightforward. I was very uncomfortable attempting to do things that I had been taught were wrong or sinful. I was always conscious of the fact that God always saw me even if no one else did. Being a very naïve individual, I thought everybody felt that way, especially if you grew up in the church.

My philosophy was that life can be difficult enough without you deliberately doing anything to make it even more difficult. After all, did not Job say that "man that is born of a woman is but a few days and full of trouble"? Why add to that trouble! Again I quickly learned that you were only labeled as boring and too saved if you dared to think and believe that way.

One good thing that resulted from my perspective of life was that I never became a victim of peer pressure. I never felt the need to be accepted or fit in at the expense of causing harm or any type of punishment to myself. From these unique differences were birthed quality as well as quantity time being alone--- not lonely, just all one with me and God. Alone in the delivery room of life with the one who made me the way I am and the only one who truly understood why I was the way I am.

I married in my late teens and we started a family shortly thereafter with me giving birth to the first of our six children. There were many overwhelming adjustments to be made to married life and being as young as I was made it even more rigorous to manage and cope.

Once again my naiveness caused me to be extremely unprepared and unequipped to effectively handle the challenging stages of adjustment that I had to endure.

In addition, my mother's only advice was, "Elaine just pray about it and do not make it worse in your mind than it really is." Even though I thought that she should have had more to tell me, that advice to pray turned out to be the best advice that she could have ever given me. Thank God for a godly mother, full of wisdom, who dared to give birth to a twelve pound infant!

For a person like me with all of my unique differences, a prayer life was the answer to my prayer! It took me a while and even some years to finally give birth to a fervent prayer life but a seed had been planted; it was conceived.

It is truly amazing how prayer completely alters your vision for purpose for the better. Prayer becomes your ultrasound device and grants you the ability to focus inwardly on what is growing inside of you. You will be able to sneak a peek at the awesome fraternal twins of strength and potential developing within you. Prayer enables you to determine the successful development and maturity of God's destiny for you. All of this is because God knows just how much of life's pressures are needed for a maximum full term birth of purpose.

So I asked myself some very self-awakening questions. "Do I dare to pray yet another prayer while struggling to continue to have the faith that God is hearing me?" "Are all these things really working for my good?" Immediately crying out, "Lord I truly love you," I was able to respond to the second question. These things are working for my good because I do love the Lord! Yes, I truly love the Lord, no doubt about it, and yes I know that I have been called according to His purpose.

So with that conviction, I P.U.S.H. (Pray Until Something Happens) with the next contraction. It is a very painful and a long contraction, a contraction of confusion and fear. Thank God for the Word of God that sustains me through this arduous ordeal. The Word that is hid in my heart reassures me that God has not given me the spirit of fear, and "I can do all things through Christ which strengthens me."

Thereafter, with each contraction I gain even more strength from the Word of God to endure yet another and another labor pain. So many times alone in the labor room of life, which I later made into my prayer closet, I found out that I was never actually alone. My Creator, Lord and Savior was always there. He never left me or forsook me.

Along with my God, I had a great Helper and Comforter in the person of the Holy Ghost who comforted me and gave me a peace that passeth all understanding.

To make sure the birthing process was not aborted by the enemy of our soul, God also appointed mentoring midwives in my life to assist me at various stages along the way. Thank God for all those spiritual birth coaches who spoke prophetically into my life causing me to remain focused on the joy of birth instead of the pains of the experiences.

So I continue to dare to give birth, even when everything I ever desired and hoped for seems to be sinking into life's quicksand. It is so easy to give in...yet not so easy to believe that you can exchange your differences for a life that you have envisioned for yourself.

Not giving up builds up a resistance. This resistance allows me to turn these differences into stepping stones of courage and faith, to become all that I know God made me to be.

Yes Lord, I had to cry out so many times with tears streaming down my face, pains in my heart, and fears in my mind. Yes Lord, "I dare to be different...Yes Lord, I dare to give birth!"

With each birthing process, I had to come to realize that a lifetime of unending sacrifices is such a small price to pay to know that God, my Creator, did not make a mistake when He created me just the way I am. It doesn't matter who does not celebrate you and your unique differences. What truly matters is that you were put here to give birth to purposes.

Steadfastly, I continue to move toward my God-given destiny with a desire and determination to become the woman and vessel that God saw in me when he formed me in my mother's belly. I am resolved to take on this challenge no matter how difficult it will be to mold my unique differences into that finished product.

Through many of my life's birthing processes, I have held on to the vision of the look that was on my father's and mother's face and the words that they possibly uttered when they both laid eyes on me for the very first time. I truly believe that God had spoken to them and had given them a glimpse in the spirit of what I was to become. Even though they both are with the Lord now, I am yet blanketed by the prayers that they stored up concerning me while they were here on earth....so I DARE TO GIVE BIRTH TO MY PURPOSES!

Dare to Give Birth and Bear Life's Pain

Finding That Truly Without, There is No Gain

Dare to P.U.S.H. Yourself Into Amazing Victories

That God Has Already Said You Can Obtain

Chapter 2
Dare to Release

In the previous chapter, we were introduced to the marriage of our God-given differences to our God-given purposes. We were made aware that from this marriage comes many births that assist in escorting us down the aisle to our destiny.

After giving birth to a large family of purposes, you will discover that it is absolutely to your advantage to nurture, develop, and mature each of them. There is a time and season for each of them to reach their full potential.

Just like with our natural children, once we have given birth to them, we choose to accept a life-time exploit of many trial and error experiences. As it is with natural children, so it is with our purposes. In spite of the ups and downs, the good, the bad and the ugly, we are committed to their care. Our purposes that we have birthed have been entrusted into our keeping and it is our God-given responsibility to be good stewards over them.

Each purpose requires your undivided spiritual attention through prayer, fasting, and an extremely devoted, consecrated life. Remember that God has already placed inside of you everything that you need to successfully and fruitfully parent the purposes that He has birthed out of you.

That is the reason why something that may be required for someone else may not necessarily work for you. Also, we must be extremely careful not to compare or measure our progress to other individuals. If quantity and quality time is required of you to develop your purposes, then that is what you must adhere to in order to perfect what has been entrusted to you.

In the natural, one of the most difficult things to do after giving birth is to release. After years of much nurturing, bonding, and sharing in every moment of a child's life, there comes a monumental time when we must release that child. We must do so in order that the child can go to an entirely new level of growing, soaring, and maturity. At the same time, there are also many benefits that you will receive as you initiate that release. Yes, releasing can be extremely difficult and sometimes even painful, but the rewards that are produced as a result of doing it far outweigh any sacrifice. Then, on the other hand, daring to release can be kind of scary and quite intimidating. It can force you to come face to face with many of life's uncertainties that you are not emotionally, mentally, or even spiritually ready for.

Remember that one of the keys to releasing is to continue to move forward while exercising extreme caution. By doing so, you will not overlook or delete any major milestones. Failing to do so can cause you to waste precious time dealing with negative and unnecessary consequences.

You must pay close attention to the speedometer of life so that you are able to gauge when you need to slow down or when it is time for full speed ahead. During these times of accelerated release, we dare to take the limits and the brakes off of our minds and wills. From there we must allow God to take complete control of all of us as we cruise through life's winding road. At this pivotal point of our lives, it is about getting out of the passenger seat and sliding over into the driver seat of destiny. Now, you will begin to ease into a new phase of releasing that allows you to become the navigator as opposed to just being a spectator to your destiny.

It is here that I must warn you that you are about to enter an amazing zone that must be approached with the utmost care. If you have successfully released everything that is required of you up to this point, then you are in for an abundant increase of growth. You are about to tap into a place where very few people ever make it or even dare to go.

It is there in that amazing zone that you discover that you are catching up with God and what he has done in you and for you, even before you were born. You will become awed at how you have been able to overcome, survive, and even thrive in the midst of ---and in spite of, some of your most challenging and devastating quests of life.

Now, you will be able to see and understand that you are just now ready to begin on the project of completing yourself that God has already finished when he created you. You can now begin to do what you once could only imagine or never thought was even possible, and that is live your life transparently. You will no longer be afraid or reluctant to allow others to share in what you have struggled through in your life and fought to keep a secret. You will want others to rejoice with you and be happy for you because of the treasures that your Creator has strategically placed inside of your earthen vessel. You will want others to join you as you begin your journey to places that you yourself never thought was possible to go; to live and enjoy life with you the way God created it to be enjoyed, and as my mother would often times say, so that you can "learn to live and live to learn."

God has declared that all that He made was good and very good! As we dare to release, we too will find ourselves agreeing that it is good! Our lives are good and very good! We only have one, so let us release ourselves to make it very good with all of our differences. It can be the best life ever lived.

Whether we have come to the realization or not, we all desire to live out to the fullest, our God-given purposes. We all have a God-ordained destiny to reach, and we each have what is required in order to make that obtainable.

With these requirements being met, we are now eligible to enroll in the higher institution of release. You will dare to graduate not once, but many times with a degree that ushers you into a position that qualifies you to assist other individuals who are striving to get where you are.

This bestows upon us the opportunity to reach back and inspire others. You will find out that each time that you release a portion of yourself you are only making room for personal growth and advancement. Has not our Creator already declared that "give and it shall be given unto you…"?

It is extremely important that we pass on to others what we have learned from our life's experiences. We must model by example and precept that daring to release is not just about letting go of someone or something, but it is about disconnecting from all of the external as well as internal distractions. These distractions could prevent you from reaching your destiny and cause you to make bad decisions.

It is very crucial that you learn to dissect each of your life's experiences, get rid of dead weight, and take what is left and make good use of it.

At this point, releasing transforms into a sort of pruning process. Sometimes it becomes necessary for you to be cut back in order for you to truly and fully flourish and blossom into your destiny. Of course, it can be a very painful and uncomfortable process, but one that always offers us a most valuable learning opportunity.

During the process of release pruning (which by the way, comes in seasons), it is vital that you remain closely connected to your survival source which is your Creator. The reason for this is so that you will not miss out on your season and time for major advancement and increase.

Speaking of seasons, have you noticed that in the beginning of the spring season there is an absolutely breathtaking assortment of blooms, both floral and foliage? They all seem to begin blossoming at about the same time. As they continue to grow into full bloom, you are yet able to distinguish each from the other. Even in a flower garden, each individual plant or flower visibly makes its own unique statement. However, if you were to release any one of these blooms from the garden, it could easily remain just as beautiful or more so on its own.

So it is with releasing. Each purpose that has been birthed out of us must be given the opportunity through releasing, to blossom fully on its own. There are times in your life that everything seems to be beautiful, so to speak. Even though we may have these seasons of beauty and bliss, that doesn't mean that we have reached our full destiny. There are always higher heights and deeper depths that God wants to take us to.

That is the reason why some individuals who feel that they are ready to retire end up refueling or recharging or awakening into one of the best seasons of their life. They had to dare to release the idea that there was nothing left for them to productively contribute to someone or something.

Sometimes life's challenges cause us to experience severe burnout and lack of drive. You may feel as if you have nothing left for yourself, much less for anyone else. It is at these times that you must dare to release the misconceptions and false information that is fed into you by the circumstances of your temporary setback!

Simultaneously, you must strive to regain your strength and new energy from one of the purposes that you have already given birth to. This must be done so that you can dare to release a clearer focus on what is really about to happen.

You must remind yourself that if you could give birth to purpose and endure the pain of it, then you can certainly survive a temporary setback. Temporary setbacks only prepare you for permanent and greater comebacks!

Just imagine the freedom that will come after you have dared to release yourself from all the unanswered questions that you have concerning your journey to your destiny. Tell yourself, "I Release Me To Be Me." Believe me, you are the only one that can hold you back!

Dare To Release, Dare to Believe

That If You Give, You Shall Receive

Countless Rewards, Afresh And Anew

Pressed Down, Shaken Together, Are Waiting For You

Chapter 3
Dare to Dance

After experiencing the freedom of daring to release, it is now time, my sisters and brothers, to dare to dance!

The shackles are off, and the ballroom floor of life has been decluttered. There are no more distractions and obstacles that can trip us up and tangle our feet. We are now free to dance away into our destiny. Do you dare to dance?

Before you dare to dance, you must first grasp the true meaning and difference between being different and daring to be different. We were all born different, but you must make a conscious and precise decision to dare to be different. The first, you have no control over or choice in the matter. The second one is left entirely up to you.

When you truly understand the difference, you have turned on the symphony inside of you that provides music for you to dare to dance by. You are now ready for your first dance lesson.

During this lesson, you will find yourself oftentimes alone with yourself dancing with the privilege of learning a lot about who you really are. While this may seem strange, believe it or not, some people are somewhat reluctant to be alone with themselves. They avoid doing so by constantly bombarding themselves and surrounding themselves with other people or temporal distractions. They do this in order to shun hearing and facing the truth about themselves.

When these people do find themselves alone, they attempt to drown out themselves with external mechanical noises and all kinds of artificial devices. They fail to realize that they are only dulling their hearing to the symphony that is requiring them to dare to dance.

They are completely ignorant of the golden moments of engrossing in the precious melodies of life's symphony that is playing deep down inside of them. They are denying themselves the pleasure of tasting and indulging in the creative juices that were poured into them by their Creator.

But oh how sweet it is when you finally allow yourself to tune into the symphony that is playing your song. It is then that you become aware of what you have been missing out on. All of a sudden you will find yourself gliding to the music. With a jolt of amazement, you will begin to ask yourself the question, "Do I dare to dance?" The answer to this question hinges on how you perceive your unique differences while you are listening to the symphony that is playing inside of you.

After successfully completing the first dance lesson, you may move on to the next one. It is the one that teaches you to dance with realization. It is the realization that even though we are born with God-given, unique differences, it is necessary at certain times to channel surf.

Channel surfing causes us to realize first of all, that it is alright to change the channel of the symphony of life that is playing inside of you. As a matter of fact, as we prance from season to season in our lives, it is extremely important that we do change channels.

Secondly, channel surfing introduces you to an assortment of dance partners. Each time that you exchange partners, you will experience being swept off of your feet into the most harmonious adventure of life.

When you discover a channel that seemingly whirls you across the obstacles that once entangled your feet, watch out! You can rest assure that the enemy of your soul will tap you on the shoulder and cut in with the intentions of interrupting and even stopping your dance.

He does this by magnifying your unique differences from a negative perspective. He desires to resurface feelings of self-condemnation, insecurity, shame, and other crippling thoughts that will disqualify you from becoming one of the best dancers ever.

His purpose for this is to take what you have learned on the dance floor of life and put it back into shackles. He is afraid of the awesome progress that you have accomplished and the new spin on life that is ahead for you.

To immediately prevent these shackles from becoming a stronghold, you must resist the enemy and he will flee... while you continue to dance!

Dance in the enemy's face. Bruise your heel on his head. Dance in spite of, because of, and in celebration of. Dance with another realization that with each unique difference comes a certain amount of courage and strength.

This courage and strength causes us to release past hurts, to relish present help, and to make us never regret the course our lives have taken! God is in control. How dare the enemy dare me NOT to dance!

There is a reason why it is extremely necessary for you to keep right on dancing after the enemy has dared you not to. When you dare to dance, you have made room on the ballroom floor of life for others to join you.

Your determination and fortitude to dance in spite of, has sent out an invitation. This invitation reads:

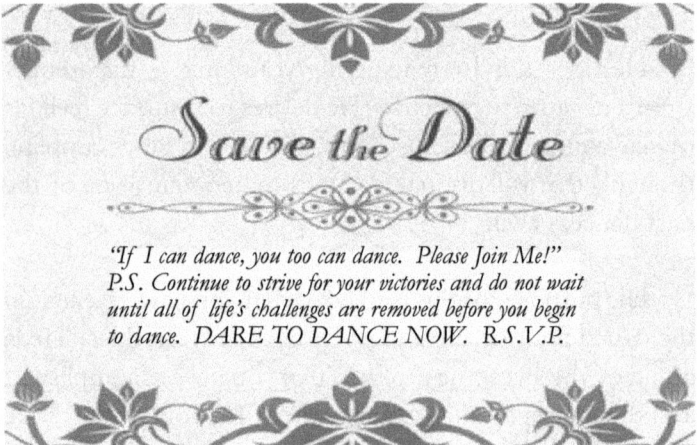

Save the Date

"If I can dance, you too can dance. Please Join Me!"
P.S. Continue to strive for your victories and do not wait until all of life's challenges are removed before you begin to dance. DARE TO DANCE NOW. R.S.V.P.

No one that has ever dared to be different would DARE to refuse this invitation. The acceptance of this invite will awaken a sleeping boldness within you. This boldness will equip you with the qualification to use the dance lessons that you have learned and take the initiative to teach many wonderful dance routines of life.

Instead of waiting to be asked to dance, you will become the one who does the asking. Ask Wisdom, "May I have this dance," when you are at the crossroads of indecision. Ask Strength, "May I have this dance," when you at your weakest point. Ask Laughter, "May I have this dance," when you are having moments of overwhelming sadness. Ask Rainbows and Sunshine, "May I have this dance," when your way is cloudy!

Most important of all, remember that God will always provide you with a partner to dance with you. You will never dance alone. God's partners of love, joy, peace, longsuffering, gentleness, meekness, faith, temperance, goodness, and many more await you. There will always be a partner there waiting on you to sweep you off of your feet and dance until times truly get better!

So dance my brother and sister! Dance with all your might! Dance like David danced! Dare To Dance!

Dare My Friend To Dance

It Could Be The Beginning Of A Great Romance

Between Your Purpose And Destiny

Hand In Hand, Oh How Beautiful It Could Be!

Chapter 4
Dare to Let Go and Let God

Now that you have finally dared to dance, you are well on your way to not only daring to be different, but deciding how you will dare to be different. It is totally up to you. Letting go and letting God helps you to decide how.

You must understand that how you let go and let God is determined by the differences that the Creator himself has placed inside of you. Our unique differences are the Creator's gauge to make sure that we are truly ready to release, allowing Him to press the fast forward button to take us to our destiny. Refusal to let go and let God can place us in an indefinite pause mode.

Our differences are a lot like fingerprints. No two sets are the same. So it is with letting go and letting God. The way that you let go and let God is not necessarily the same way that the Creator has ordered for someone else. One size does not fit all in this case. If it does not fit, it is due to the fact that it has not been designed especially for you.

When you dare to let go and let God, you are approaching and are closer than ever before to graduating from life's highest institution of experience, that is the school of hard knocks.

Letting go and letting God means that you have finally learned from all of life's hard knocks (and believe me, there are many) that there are some things you must just let go! Let it go. Stop worrying about it; stop rehearsing it and nursing it; stop trying to fix it and make it work. Just let it go!

Usually by the time you graduate, you are completely exhausted and burnt out, not from the hard knocks, but from the process of learning to truly let go and let God. It is not until we really learn to let go that God will allow us to experience the real benefits of daring to be different. Your differences will help you to decide just what you need to let go of and how to let it go.

Some things you must let go of...cold turkey! There will be no more need for further prayer or attempting to seek counseling concerning it. It will be time for immediate action.

For other dilemmas you must learn to let go of the confusion and burden of carrying them. The only way to do this is to seek God whole-heartedly for directives instead of trying to find even more ways to procrastinate about letting them go.

Now you must learn to let go of any temptations to mentally harbor any negative thoughts. This is harmful and will prevent God from allowing you to move on to your destiny. You certainly do not want to go backwards and pick up anything that you have let go of. Letting go is the first real beginning of becoming not just healed, but completely whole!

I will let you in on a little secret. The harder it is to make the decision to let go is an indication that there is no other way around it. So let go and let God. Usually the decision to let go is so difficult because it is due to the inability to let go of the "disease to please". Once you are cured of that, you will find that it becomes easier to let go.

No doubt some of you are at the point where I once was, wondering, "But how do I let go?" First, let me just say that it is so amazing how we can become extremely attached to things that really mean us absolutely no good. It is a very important question (How do I let go?) and no one but you can answer that question when you are faced with it. Of course, your Creator will be there to guide you along and assist you in getting the answer.

The answer may at first seem complicated, but it really is quite simple. The truth of the matter is that we let go by letting God, and we let God by letting go. I know…you are even more confused!

So let me put it this way. We must make a conscious effort to allow God to do what He wants to do for us. We do this by first letting go of whatever we are holding on to.

You see, God will never do for us what He has given us the power and ability to do, and at the same time, He will not force anything from us that we are holding on to in order to give us something better. We hold God back and rob Him of the opportunity to give us His best when we hold on to whatever it is that we won't let go of.

You must understand that it is not necessarily a physical letting go but oftentimes it is a letting go of the fear of the unknown or the outcome. In this case, if it is fear, when we let go of it (mainly because "God has NOT given us the spirit of fear") then it is like giving Him the permission to bestow upon us the courage that we need. We should not be holding on to anything that He has not given us.

It is our nature to want and hold on to what we want. Letting go, on the other hand, is about exchanging what we want for what God wants for us.

In our Creator's divine plan for us, there are some things that He will not give to us until we first let go of something. It is like getting rid of the junk in order to make room for the valuable treasures. Really, it boils down to a matter of completely and unquestionably trusting God!

So how does daring to be different fit into all of this? Well the differences that the Creator has placed inside of you are just what you need to trust Him and let go of whatever is holding you back.

You are an original and not a carbon copy of anyone else on the face of this earth. What you ultimately let go of will totally define all the wonderful you,that you are . You should be inspired to let go of whatever is holding you back from becoming that wonderful individual that you truly are.

Your differences are designed to bring you closer to your destiny as well as to enable you to make a one-of-a-kind difference in this world.

No one can do what you have been created to do and how you were created to do it. We must ultimately let go of the temptation and struggles to change ourselves. You must learn to let God be in full control and in charge of the changes that he wants to make for you and in you!

Dare To Let Go And Let God

What Is It That Is Keeping You Apart

From Drawing Nigh To Your Maker

He Has Drawn Nigh To You

Now, He Is Waiting Patiently For You

To Come To Him Too!

Chapter 5
Dare to be All One

Oh to spend quality and quantity time with the ALMIGHTY ONE.......

A – Almighty
L – Lovingly
O – Ordering
N – Navigating
E – Every Step

The society we live in today has unfortunately dictated to us that when it comes to making life's most important decisions we only have two options from which to choose. They have made us feel that we are only allowed to make one or the other and never both at the same time. Simply put, these choices are quality or quantity.

Because the majority of society has made the wrong choices in many cases, it has caused a massive decline in our foundational and structured institutions of life. Not to mention that these wrong choices have caused many people to find themselves completely alone. This is due to the fact that most successful decisions of life require quality as well as quantity.

When we neglect to give life's most important and meaningful building blocks both quality and quantity, we inevitably find ourselves focusing excessively and unhealthily on self.

God never intended for man to be an island or alone, but instead He meant for each of us to be All-ONE with Him.

First of all, becoming all one with our Creator can only be achieved by spending quality as well as quantity time with Him. He in turn, will place people around you with various differences that will invest both quality and quantity time and resources into you.

For you see our differences enrich each other's lives and teach us so much about making it in this world. Each of us must reach back and teach someone about what life has taught us. I need you, and you need me. We must be careful that we do not take what we have received from being all one with God and not pass it on with quality and quantity to others.

Loneliness, feelings of hopelessness, anxiety, and fear (just to name a few) are all the results of spending too much negative quality and quantity time on yourself.

Even while we are experiencing these negative feelings, we tend to nurse them by isolating and pulling back from other people. This is not healthy. These are the times that we should and must struggle to fight through the temptation to remain at that place of isolation.

It is critical to force yourself to nurture your relationship with your maker instead of pampering your negative feelings while being alone. This is absolutely the time to really become all one with Him, and He will without a doubt assign the right people with the right differences to your life crisis.

These individuals will patiently give you their quality and quantity attention until you are strong and have fully recovered. When you have become healed and whole, then you will be able to invest quality and quantity into countless others. God will allow you to be the most effective you can be with all of your unique differences.

Everything that God has spoken to you while you are ALL ONE with Him, others who have been assigned to you by Him will echo and reemphasize the same as they pour into you. This will reaffirm your differences and how God wants to ultimately use them.

You will gradually, but surely regain your confidence and strength to remain steadfast in your fight to become all that God has purposed for you to be and to Dare To Be Different.

There will be times and even prolonged seasons when you will find yourself uncomfortable in your comfort zone. There will also be seasons when all that you thought you could not live without will be peeled back away from you. You will feel as if you are all alone in this world and that no one has come even close to experiencing anything like what you are going through.

There will also be other seasons in your life when your weeping has endured for a night and yet another night…and there is no morning seemingly in sight, much less any joy.

It doesn't matter how high one's self esteem may be, sometimes there comes a time in all of our lives when we do not feel up and ready to tackle life's challenges and/or the false evidence that the only thing that we can expect out of life is nothing in return for all the trials and tribulations that we have come into and have gone through! Sometimes we feel just plain weary in well doing, all alone and forgotten.

But when you discover yourself at one of these places, you are at the right place to become even richer and better than you have ever been before. God has promised us that He would supply each and every need that you find yourself in need of according to his riches in Glory. You are at a wealthy place in Him!

So we must come to realize that our greatest need is to be ALL ONE with HIM. When this happens, He, our ultimate provider, will fill any void that you or I may have – no matter how long we have had it and no matter how deep it is…

Dare To Be ALL-ONE With Him

Let Him Your Life Fulfill

Put Him In The Center

And You Will Thrive Within!

Chapter 6
Dare to Face the Truth

Have you ever wondered why it is that in the midst of our most devastating situations and circumstances of life that we find it extremely difficult to face and handle the truth?

There is an old saying that includes, "You may fool some of the people some of the time..." My addition to that cliché is that you can't fool yourself any of the time. That is the case because truth has a way of hanging around with the patience of Job until we own up to it.

We may delay, but we can't deny that the truth is just the truth, and it doesn't change or go away simply because we want it to. Nonetheless, I must admit that we give it our best shot trying to fool ourselves by avoiding the truth.

One of the main ways that we attempt to get around the truth is by playing the oldest game since the world as we know it began. That old game is called the old blame game.

We tend to blame everything and everybody because we are unable to face the truth. It is utterly impossible to move forward with our lives after a major devastation or setback while playing this game. When we persistently attempt to do this, we are failing to realize that we are only pressing the pause button or the rewind button of life. Simultaneously, we declare that we want nothing more than to be able to move on with our lives. But once again, it is simply impossible unless we dare to face the truth.

The very thing that you are having so much difficulty facing (which, by the way is the truth) is the very thing that will thrust you into fulfilling your God-given purpose and usher you into your destiny.

The truth is, daring to face the truth releases a giant of courage within you. This courage will permit you to see circumstances from an entirely new set of perspectives.

Actually, for the first time in your life, you may begin to see yourself from a giant's perspective of being on top instead of at the bottom. You will no longer exhaust precious energy and effort seeking out the opinions of others concerning directives for your own life. You will take charge of your own destiny. You will experience yourself taking on a proactive attitude to help bring your destiny to pass.

Daring to face the truth will truly turn on the light and allow you to see who you really are and what the Creator has created inside of you. It will be like looking in the mirror and seeing the reflection of someone who is very capable of doing great exploits.

Facing the truth will not only give you the courage to leap forward, but you also get a glimpse of a flicker of light at the end of the tunnel; that tunnel that was once only darkness and had been for a very long time.

Ah! For you see truth is light! It will enlighten you to a whole new way of life ahead that is waiting for you to just face the truth.

Once you have finally faced the truth, it will dawn on you that the differences that God has designed you with are more than enough for you to finish another chapter of your life. From there you can move on to yet another and another amazing and adventurous chapter of your life.

God has placed inside of you and around you exactly what you need to obtain the things you deserve. You must make the most of what you presently have.

However, there is a red flag that you should beware of when it comes to daring to face the truth. Always be mindful of the fact that truth comes in an assortment of packages. It can arrive in a variety of shapes and sizes. It can also be delivered to you when you are least expecting it or you are not quite prepared to receive it.

Truth can catch you off guard by arriving C.O.D. When this happens you may find yourself unprepared or unwilling to pay the price of accepting the truth. Then, there are times when we will try to determine by the outside of the packaging in which the truth arrives whether or not we can handle what awaits us inside. Quite frankly, due to the challenges of life, the package containing the truth can sometimes reach us in a battered and unattractive condition.

Once again, we may find ourselves attempting to alter the truth, rearrange the truth, or even hide the truth. We may fail to recognize the truth for what it is worth.

What you may not be aware of is that the truth becomes even more valuable and necessary to face as time passes by. It does not depreciate with time just because we continue to ignore it. Truth will constantly scream out to you declaring that it will not be ignored and it cannot be ignored. You can stumble over it, turn a deaf ear to it, and even disrobe it, only to discover that what you have is just the plain naked truth.

You may toss that old battered and torn package of truth aside with the hopes that maybe with time there will be no need to face the real truth. On the contrary, you will find out that life circumstances just continue to deliver to you even more of those same kinds of truth packages. Instead of facing it, you continue to brainstorm over and over again about how to avoid it.

You will at some point have to face the fact that no matter the packaging, until you open up to the truth and face it, it will continue to be stamped.....RETURN TO SENDER . As a result, these packages will just continue to pile up in the dead letter pile.

Your journey of life will be put on hold until you dare to face the truth. You will find yourself at the exact same place after much time has passed you by. This will happen until you stop and ask yourself, "Why sit here and die?!"

There is a secret to rising up, becoming proactive like never before, and finally facing the truth. After this, you will no longer want to ignore the truth, hide the truth, avoid the truth, or cover up or deny the truth.

The secret and the truth is that the truth is already inside of you. That is the reason that you can never avoid it, ignore it, or outlive it.

This is also why sometimes it comes battered and in all kinds of troublesome conditions. Delaying facing the truth that is already inside of you can take a toll on you. Because no matter what you have gone through, when it's all said and done you know the truth behind every circumstance. You have to just dare to face the truth.

You can't outrun yourself. You have no choice but to live with yourself as long as you are in this world. Most of all you cannot "fool yourself any of the time." So dare to face the truth; dare to face yourself and what you are most afraid of. You can and you will make it!

DARE TO FACE THE TRUTH

No Matter How It Arrives

Dressed Or Naked, It Will Most

Certainly Survive!

Chapter 7
Dare to Think the Unthinkable

I dare you to begin thinking of accomplishing something positive and challenging that you may have once convinced yourself that you are incapable of doing.

There are countless numbers of books, sayings, and popular clichés about positive thinking and the power behind it. You have probably heard of and read them all, so I will not bore you with any of them. However, it has been proven that you can think yourself into anything as well as think yourself out of anything, but I would like to challenge you to dare to think the unthinkable!

First of all, if you dare, ask yourself what is the difference between people who think that they can do anything they set their minds to and the people who are just plain afraid to do much thinking at all?

To me there is something so wonderfully intriguing and thought-provoking about the power and ability to think. Just to meditate on that thought can open up an entirely new world of things that will begin to change for you in your life.

Secondly, it is so extremely amazing how each of us can think as much and as long as we would like without even the person in the same room with us ever knowing it.

Whether those thoughts are negative or positive, unless you act those thoughts out, no one except God of course, will ever know what you are thinking. Have you ever [THOUGHT] of that?

The world of thoughts is truly awesome!

It is our thoughts that will allow us to escape mentally and emotionally from life's share of traumas long before our physical bodies catch up. So it is in that captivating world of thoughts, that we can achieve what seems to be impossible, reach the unreachable, touch the intangible, and see the invisible. The possibilities become limitless when all of our thoughts begin to work together and we dare to think the unthinkable.

At some point of understanding we come to know that the ability to think and the power of collecting and processing thoughts comes from God, our Creator. That awareness causes us to comprehend the actuality that God in His divine plan and purpose for us has a distinctive reason why He enables us to think, especially the unthinkable.

By now you are probably wondering, what are the unthinkables? From my experience, I have discovered the answer to that question. Simply put, the unthinkables are those thoughts that you dare not think about. You dare not think about them because they force you to confront and deal with the challenges that will cause you to stretch yourself beyond what you will consider to be normal for you. When you dare to think the unthinkable you have compelled yourself to accept the possibility of grasping a whole new set of normals.

Thinking the unthinkable brings to surface those unimaginable endeavors that you never envisioned for yourself. The unthinkables will broaden your perspective of your unique differences and present you with a bird's eye view of you without limitations. You will begin to see yourself as a high achiever instead of measuring yourself only by where you are now. Instead, you will challenge yourself to expand past yourself.

Now let us compare for a moment thinking to dreaming. You can have and enjoy the most amazing dream. Everything concerning that dream can appear to be so realistic and exciting. Yet, after a period of time of having a dream, you will awake. After awakening, sometimes the recollection of that dream will vanish from your memory bank and you will be unable to recall the events of that dream.

That dream may return at some point, but there is no guarantee that it will. Even if later you are able to recall and rehearse the happenings of the dream that doesn't necessarily mean that it will come to pass. In other words, unfortunately, sometimes even good dreams die.

But on the other hand, thinking is like planting seeds. The more we think, the more that seed of thought is watered and cultivated. Thoughts, like well-nurtured seeds, will grow and grow. Even negative seeds of thought will grow so beware of what you plant in your thought garden.

Some of the most outstanding and lifetime achievements started out (not as a dream) but as a thought. Remember the story of the little engine…oops, I said I wasn't going to bore you with any of those stories!

The reason some of the greatest accomplishments are started with the seed of thought is because our highest level of performance is done while we dare to think the unthinkable.

Now let's go back and take another look at dreaming for a brief moment. You may have a dream that continues for only a short time while you are asleep. On the other hand, thoughts can go on long after you have awakened, and they continue to live and thrive for hours and hours. Even while you are engaged in other activities throughout the day, your thoughts can yet be at work. Thinking allows you to be employed on at least two jobs at the same time.

Ahh….! It just dawned on me the reason why the Holy Spirit inspired Apostle Paul to pen these words…."Finally brethren, whatsoever things are true, whatsoever things are honest, whatsoever things are just, whatsoever things are pure, whatsoever things are lovely, whatsoever things are of good report; if there be any virtue, and if there be any praise, THINK on these things."

My own personal interpretation of that verse is that you must, "Dare to think the unthinkable." Let's use just one word of the verse for an example if I may. It seems unthinkable for you to dare to think about things that are lovely when you are coping with unlovely situations, circumstances, or people. Then again, it is at this time that you should ask yourself a very serious question. "What is it in me that makes me different and will cause me to think on lovely things when someone else will focus only on the unlovely?" Also, remember that your thoughts are like seeds; they do grow. So if you think lovely, you will grow lovely.

As I mentioned earlier, my mother would oftentimes say to me while I was in the midst of unlovely situations of life, "Elaine don't make it worse in your MIND than it is." You can add that to your list of popular positive thinking quotes!

And oh how true it is. If we would only take a moment to think before we actually think, we will discover that it is truly not as bad as we have made it out to be. That is why I believe God gave us the power to retain memories. There are times that we need to remind ourselves not to be so hasty in what we are thinking.

Daring to think the unthinkable provokes you to sift through the rubbish of all of your broken pieces of thoughts, then piece them back together in your mind and begin to see a portrait of purpose and destiny.

Daring to think the unthinkable stretches your faith to believe for unlimited impossibilities. It will give you the patience to accept the truth, the comfort during extremely difficult times in your life, and cause you to force a little smile across your face when sadness floods your heart.

Daring to think the unthinkable will cause you to Give Birth To Your Purposes, Dare To Release, Dare To Dance, Dare To Let Go And Let God, Dare To Become All One With Him, and Dare To Face The Truth!

Last but not least, daring to think the unthinkable puts another day of challenge behind you, places you another day closer to your earthly goals that your Creator has ordained for you, and draws you nearer to your eternal destiny and victory.

So begin to Dare To Be Different and to think yourself into knowing that The Best Is Yet To Come!

Dare To Think The Unthinkable

Dare To Trust Your Mind

To Protect All The Golden Nuggets

That Your Thoughts Have Left Behind!

Dare To Be Different

Dare To Stand Alone

Dare to Go With Others Who Are Daring To Be Strong

Dare To Make A Difference, So Someone Else Can See

That Daring To Be Different Is The Place

They Too Would Love To Be!

Chapter 8
Dare to Begin Again...

This chapter in itself is different. It is unique because after reading this book it is now the beginning of the dawning of a new day for you. It is no accident or coincidence that you have chosen and been inspired to read this book.

It is also not happenstance that God moved upon me to write only seven chapters. The eighth has been reserved for you to go over and beyond the perfect number of completion and step into a new era of your own life. There is a book inside of you that was begun the day that you were conceived. I dare you to begin again . . .

To be continued by you..........

Dare To Begin Again

Take A Long Look Within

At Something Brighter, Something

Much Stronger

Don't you DARE Put It Off

Any Longer!!!

Write Your Vision Make it Plain

Write Your Vision Make it Plain

_____

_____

_____

_____

_____

_____

_____

_____

_____

_____

_____

_____

_____

_____

_____

_____

_____

_____

_____

Write Your Vision Make it Plain

_____

_____

_____

_____

_____

_____

_____

_____

_____

_____

_____

_____

_____

_____

_____

_____

_____

_____

_____

Write Your Vision Make it Plain

_____
_____
_____
_____
_____
_____
_____
_____
_____
_____
_____
_____
_____
_____
_____
_____
_____
_____
_____
_____

Write Your Vision Make it Plain

_____

_____

_____

_____

_____

_____

_____

_____

_____

_____

_____

_____

_____

_____

_____

_____

_____

_____

_____

Write Your Vision Make it Plain

_____

_____

_____

_____

_____

_____

_____

_____

_____

_____

_____

_____

_____

_____

_____

_____

_____

_____

_____

Write Your Vision Make it Plain

_____

_____

_____

_____

_____

_____

_____

_____

_____

_____

_____

_____

_____

_____

_____

_____

_____

_____

Write Your Vision Make it Plain

_____
_____
_____
_____
_____
_____
_____
_____
_____
_____
_____
_____
_____
_____
_____
_____
_____
_____
_____

Write Your Vision Make it Plain

_____

_____

_____

_____

_____

_____

_____

_____

_____

_____

_____

_____

_____

_____

_____

_____

_____

Write Your Vision Make it Plain

_____

_____

_____

_____

_____

_____

_____

_____

_____

_____

_____

_____

_____

_____

_____

_____

_____

_____

_____

Write Your Vision Make it Plain

Write Your Vision Make it Plain

_____

_____

_____

_____

_____

_____

_____

_____

_____

_____

_____

_____

_____

_____

_____

_____

_____

_____

_____

Write Your Vision Make it Plain

_____

_____

_____

_____

_____

_____

_____

_____

_____

_____

_____

_____

_____

_____

_____

_____

_____

_____

_____

Write Your Vision Make it Plain

_____

_____

_____

_____

_____

_____

_____

_____

_____

_____

_____

_____

_____

_____

_____

_____

Write Your Vision Make it Plain

_____

_____

_____

_____

_____

_____

_____

_____

_____

_____

_____

_____

_____

_____

_____

_____

_____

_____

Write Your Vision Make it Plain

_____

_____

_____

_____

_____

_____

_____

_____

_____

_____

_____

_____

_____

_____

_____

_____

_____

_____

_____

Write Your Vision Make it Plain

_____

_____

_____

_____

_____

_____

_____

_____

_____

_____

_____

_____

_____

_____

_____

_____

_____

_____

_____

Write Your Vision Make it Plain

_____

_____

_____

_____

_____

_____

_____

_____

_____

_____

_____

_____

_____

_____

_____

_____

_____

_____

Write Your Vision Make it Plain

Write Your Vision Make it Plain

_____

_____

_____

_____

_____

_____

_____

_____

_____

_____

_____

_____

_____

_____

_____

_____

_____

_____

_____

Write Your Vision Make it Plain

_____

_____

_____

_____

_____

_____

_____

_____

_____

_____

_____

_____

_____

_____

_____

_____

_____

_____

Write Your Vision Make it Plain

_____

_____

_____

_____

_____

_____

_____

_____

_____

_____

_____

_____

_____

_____

_____

_____

_____

www.ingramcontent.com/pod-product-compliance
Lightning Source LLC
Chambersburg PA
CBHW052204090426
42741CB00010B/2407